FRANCE

Annabel Warrender and Michael Cotsell

Illustrated by Joseph McEwan

Designed by Graham Round

Edited by Jenny Tyler and Angela Wilkes

Contents

The name Usborne and the device are
Trade Marks of Usborne Publishing Ltd.

Additional artwork by Roger Mann.

First published in 1979 by
Usborne Publishing Ltd,
20 Garrick Street, London WC2E 9BJ, England.
Printed in Belgium by Henri Proost
& Cie pvba, Turnhout.

How to Use this Book

This is a picture guide book packed with information about France. Take it on holiday with you and find out about lots of exciting things to see and do, or read it at home and find out what it is like in France.

It is a good idea to check with a local tourist office for opening times, admission fees and directions. Some places are closed during the winter and many are closed at least one day a week.

This book explains some of the new and strange sights, tells you what to eat and where to go, and suggests some fun things to do, such as going to puppet shows, watching people make wine or going ice-skating. It makes visits to châteaux and churches fun by telling you about things to spot in them. You can also find out about French shops and money.

Before you start your trip, collect as much information as you can about the area you are going to visit. There is a list of useful addresses and books on page 61. Don't forget to take your camera, a notebook for recording interesting things you see and do and coloured pencils for playing the numberplate game on page 60. Try to learn the French words for things you are specially interested in, so you will be able to ask about them when you get there.

There are lots of interesting things to spot. When you see something, put a tick in the little square next to the picture. You might be able to spot some things without even going to France, so keep your eyes open.

It is a good idea to save bus, Métro and entrance tickets, paper bags, sweet wrappers and anything else you can find so you can make a collection to remind you of your holiday. You probably won't be able to afford to save many coins, but you can make rubbings of them by putting them under a piece of paper and rubbing with a soft pencil or wax crayon, like this.

The map on page 5 shows many of the places mentioned in this book. For smaller places, the name of the *département* is given in brackets next to the name. You will find all the *départements* on the map on page 60.

Facts about France

The official name for France is La République Française. It is the largest country in Europe covering 551,500sq.km. It is hexagonal in shape and joins on to six other countries.

Divisions of France

France was divided into *départements* in 1790. Each has a number and most are named after the main river running through them. There are 95 *départements* in mainland France. Each has a main town and a *Préfet* chosen by the President.

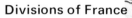

Government

The President appoints a Prime Minister and other ministers. They are responsible to Parliament, which consists of two houses, the National Assembly and the Senate. The National Assembly is elected by the people for 5 years. The Senate is elected for 9 years by local councillors.

Main products

France is the largest agricultural nation in Europe. Its main crops are: sugar beet, wheat, potatoes and barley. France and Italy share the title of world's top wine producer and France is also the second world producer of cheese, and the leading producer of perfume. Main exports are motor vehicles especially Renault, Citroen and Peugeot. More than one car in ten of total world output is French.

The President

France's last king (Louis-Philippe) abdicated in 1848. The Head of State is now the President, who is elected every seven years by the French people. Since 1981 the President has been François Mitterrand.

The flag

This has been the French flag since the French Revolution in 1789. It is called the Tricolore and is made up of the red and blue colours of Paris and the white of the Bourbon kings.

Language

French is derived from Latin spoken by Roman Legionaries. The Breton language is still sometimes used in Brittany and the Basque language in the Pyrenees.

Facts and figures

Population of France: 53,838,000
Five largest cities:
Paris   Lille
Lyon   Bordeaux
Marseille
Longest river: River Loire, 1,012km
Highest mountain: Mont Blanc, 4,807m

English Channel (La Manche)

NORD
Belgium
Lille
Luxembourg
West Germany
PICARDIE (Picardy)
• Beauvais
Bayeux
CHAMPAGNE-ARDENNES
LORRAINE
NORMANDIE (Normandy)
ILE-DE-FRANCE
Paris • Épernay
ALSACE
Chartres •
• Le Mans
River Seine
FRANCHE-COMTÉ
River Loire
CENTRE
BOURGOGNE (Burgundy)
PAYS DE LA LOIRE
• Chinon
Besançon •
Switzerland
Atlantic Ocean
POITOU-CHARENTES
Vichy •
Évian
SAVOIE
Bay of Biscay
LIMOUSIN
PÉRIGORD
Lyon •
Bordeaux
AUVERGNE
RHÔNE-ALPES
Italy
AQUITAINE
MIDI-PYRÉNÉES
PROVENCE-CÔTE D'AZUR
• Avignon
MONACO
• Bayonne
LANGUEDOC-ROUSSILLON
Marseille
Nice •
Monte Carlo
Toulouse •
• Grasse
Carcassonne •
CAMARGUE
BÉARN
Mediterranean Sea
Spain

Public holidays

1 January: *le jour de l'an*
*Easter Monday: *le lundi de Pâques*
1 May: *le premier mai*
*Ascension Day: *l'Ascension*
*Whit Monday: *le lundi de la Pentecôte*
14 July: *le 14 juillet*

15 August: *la fête de l'Assomption*
1 November: *la fête de la Toussaint (All Saint's Day)*
11 November: *le 11 novembre (Armistice Day)*
25 December: *Noel*
*Dates change each year.

5

Money

French money, the franc, is made up of 100 centimes. You can find out how much the franc is worth in pounds or dollars at any bank.

On the **100 franc note** there is a picture of Corneille, a dramatist.

The **50 franc note** shows the head of Jean Racine, a 17th century French dramatist.

The **10 franc note** has recently been changed and made smaller. The new one shows Berlioz, the composer.

Here are the French coins. Learn to recognize them so you do not make mistakes in shops.

5 centimes

5 francs
(1 franc and ½ franc coins are similar, but smaller.)

10 centimes

10 francs

20 centimes

Shopping and Eating

When you are abroad, it is fun to go round the shops and see the different kinds of things they sell. Here you can see some of the most useful places to shop. On the next page you can find out what all the smaller shops sell.

Outside most large towns there are enormous, new **shopping centres** with their own car parks. You can buy anything you want there, from food to furniture, and everything is cheaper than it is in smaller shops.

Most towns have a **market** once or twice a week in the main square. You can buy fresh food there and may even see live rabbits and chickens for sale.

The **department stores** in France are fun to look around. Other good places to shop are the cheap chain stores, such as *Monoprix* and *Prisunic*. Look for these signs.

Where to eat

Cafés are a very important part of French life. You can go there to drink or meet your friends. They are open from early in the morning until late at night.

A café called a **brasserie** sells draught beer. The word "brasserie" means brewery. You can often get simple meals and snacks in them too.

France has some of the most famous, expensive **restaurants** in the world, such as Maxim's in Paris. But there are many good, inexpensive restaurants.

Look out for signs like this along main roads. **Les Routiers** (lorry drivers') restaurants are open to everyone and serve good food at reasonable prices.

The Shops

Maison de la Presse. You can buy comics, newspapers, maps and paperbacks here.

Papeterie. This is a stationer's shop. It sells writing paper and everything children need for school.

Librairie. This is a book shop, not a library.

Tabac. Tobacconist's where you can also buy stamps and sweets. Look for the red sign.

Confiserie. This is a rather expensive kind of sweet shop.

Pâtisserie. You can buy pastries and cakes here. Sometimes there is a tea-room as well.

Boulangerie. You can buy fresh bread here. The bakery is often at the back of the shop.

You can buy chips and drinks from the **frites (chips) van.**

Vans and stalls sell **crêpes,** pancakes with lots of different fillings.

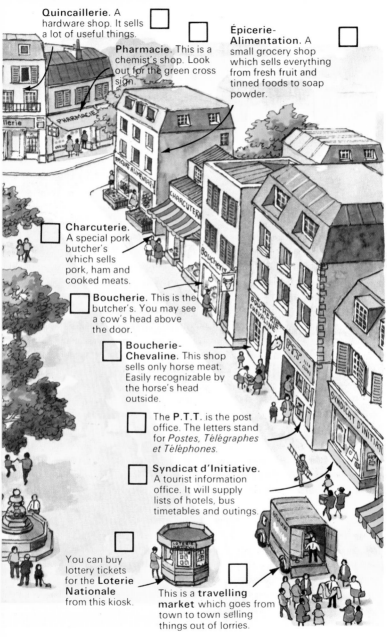

Quincaillerie. A hardware shop. It sells a lot of useful things.

Pharmacie. This is a chemist's shop. Look out for the green cross sign.

Épicerie-Alimentation. A small grocery shop which sells everything from fresh fruit and tinned foods to soap powder.

Charcuterie. A special pork butcher's which sells pork, ham and cooked meats.

Boucherie. This is the butcher's. You may see a cow's head above the door.

Boucherie-Chevaline. This shop sells only horse meat. Easily recognizable by the horse's head outside.

The **P.T.T.** is the post office. The letters stand for *Postes, Télégraphes et Téléphones*.

Syndicat d'Initiative. A tourist information office. It will supply lists of hotels, bus timetables and outings.

You can buy lottery tickets for the **Loterie Nationale** from this kiosk.

This is a **travelling market** which goes from town to town selling things out of lorries.

9

French Food

France is famous for its food and drink. The French have always taken food seriously and are very good cooks. Try to eat as many different things as you can. Here are some dishes to look out for and try.

Most of the **oysters** eaten in Europe come from Brittany. They are served in their shells and eaten raw.

Mussels (*moules*) are sometimes eaten raw. But they are often cooked and served in a white wine sauce.

Snails (*escargots*) are a great delicacy. They are served in their shells and eaten with a special fork.

Frogs' legs taste a bit like chicken. They are usually lightly fried and you eat them with your fingers.

Homard à l'armoricaine is a lobster dish from Brittany. The lobster is served in a spicy tomato sauce.

Boeuf bourguignon is a famous stew from Burgundy. It is made from beef cooked in red Burgundy wine.

Cassoulet comes from the south-west of France. It is a stew made from white beans and goose, duck or sausage meat.

Bouillabaisse is a speciality of Provence. It is a fish soup which may contain over 20 different kinds of fish.

Quiche lorraine comes from Lorraine. It is a delicious open tart filled with eggs, cream and bacon.

Salade niçoise is a speciality of Nice. It is a salad of olives, anchovies, tomatoes, onions and tuna fish.

Pâté de foie gras is a rich pâté made from goose liver and often stuffed with a rare fungus called truffles.

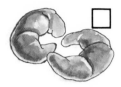

A **baguette** is the famous long French loaf with a crisp crust. You must eat it soon after it is baked.

Croissants are flaky, crescent-shaped rolls. People eat them for breakfast and often dip them into their coffee.

Brioches are a kind of sweet, soft bread bun, usually shaped like a small cottage loaf.

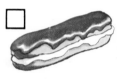

A **petit pain au chocolat** is a small flaky pastry roll with chocolate in the middle. Children eat them for tea.

Éclair. One of the most famous French pastries. Usually filled with a specially flavoured cream.

Crêpes. These pancakes are a speciality of Brittany. They can have sweet or savoury fillings.

Herbs and flavourings

Onions are used a lot in cooking and many are grown around Roscoff in Brittany. They are sold by travelling **onion sellers** on bikes.

Bay leaves and garlic are used to add flavour to dishes. You will often see **bay trees** outside restaurants.

A French meal

French people eat their main meal at midday, when they have a two-hour lunch-break. They usually start the meal with soup or crudités (raw salad vegetables). Next they have a meat or fish course. They often eat their vegetables or green salad after this. They finish the meal with cheese, then fruit or pudding.

Wine, Cheese and Newspapers

France is famous for making good wine. There are several wine growing areas and each one produces a different kind of wine. You can tell where a wine comes from by the shape of its bottle. Here are the main ones to spot.

Champagne

Burgundy

Bordeaux Alsace Côtes de Provence

Wine labels

You can find out a lot about the wine in a bottle from its label. Here are some of the things it tells you.

The year it was made (vintage).

The vineyard owner.

Bottled at the place where it was made.

CHATEAU BELAIR

SAINT EMILION
Appellation Saint Emilion
Controlée
1959
Edouard Dubois Challon
Propriétaire à Saint Emilion
MIS EN BOUTEILLES AU CHATEAU

The name of the estate.

The area the wine comes from.

Appellation Contrôlée means that the wine is good. Strict A.C. regulations control where wines come from and how they are made.

Other drinks

An apéritif is drunk before a meal to whet your appetite. **Pernod** tastes of aniseed and is very popular.

Cognac and **Kirsch** are drunk after meals. Cognac is brandy and Kirsch is a liqueur made from cherries.

Chartreuse is a green liqueur made from herbs and honey. Monks used to make it and still control how it is made.

French beer usually tastes like lager. Most of it is made in Alsace, where a lot of hops are grown.

Cider is made in Normandy and Brittany, where there are many orchards. You can buy it at supermarkets.

The main French bottled mineral waters are **Évian**, which is still, and **Perrier**, which is fizzy.

Newspapers and magazines

It is fun to look at all the different newspapers, magazines and comics when you are in France. Here are the main ones to look out for.

Le Monde and Le Figaro are the two main national daily papers. People either receive them by post or buy them at news stands or shops as there are no paper boys.

You will see a lot of weekly news magazines, such as **Paris Match,** and women's magazines, such as **Elle. Pif** is one of a big range of weekly comics.

Cheese

France makes over 350 different kinds of cheese, and every area has its specialities. Cheese goes well with wine and the French often finish a meal with cheese and fruit, rather than with pudding. Here are some cheeses for you to try.

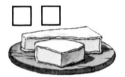

Brie and **Camembert** are round cheeses with a soft, creamy centre and a smooth white powdery crust.

Roquefort is a strong blue-veined cheese made from ewes' milk and left to mature in caves in Languedoc.

Fromage au Marc de Raisin is a round, sweet cream cheese rolled in a crust of grape seeds.

Chèvre is strongly flavoured goats' milk cheese. It is sometimes wrapped in straw and vine leaves.

Petit Suisse is a creamy, non-salted cheese, rather like smooth cottage cheese.

What to See and Do in Paris 1

Here are some things to spot on the streets of Paris, the capital of France and the fifth largest city in the world. Paris grew up along the banks of the River Seine over 2,000 years ago, and has been a centre for scholars and artists since the Middle Ages. Clues to the city's long history can be seen in the old churches, monuments and palaces lining the busy streets.

Some old Métro stations have **decorated ironwork entrances** in the *Art Nouveau* style, popular in the early 1900s.

Shops and businesses often had **picture signs** to show what they sold or made. You can still see some.

Wrought-iron was often used for decoration. Look out for **double-sided benches** like this one.

This is an **advertisement column.** Since 1881, it has been against the law to stick posters on the walls.

Wallace Fountain. One of a hundred drinking fountains given to Paris in the 1800s by an Englishman called Sir Richard Wallace.

This is a **pissoir,** or street lavatory for men. They are a rare sight now, as they are being replaced by modern inside toilets.

Plaques on walls show where famous people once lived or important events took place.

There are many different kinds of **street lamps** in Paris. Some of the more elaborate ones date back to the time when gas street lighting was first introduced. See how many you can spot.

Street life

The **Bouquinistes** have open-air stalls on the banks of the Seine. They sell old books, maps and pictures.

There are many **street painters** in Montmartre. Famous artists like Renoir and Picasso once lived here.

On the Ile de la Cité there is a **flower market** every day except Sunday, when there is a bird market instead.

There is a **bird market** on the Quai de la Mégisserie. Birds used to be set free when the king came to Paris.

The Flea Market, at the Porte de Clignancourt, sells old clothes, antique furniture and junk.

On fine days you may see a **pavement artist** like this one. When it rains, his picture will be washed away.

Pavement cafés are a common Paris sight. Notice the waiters with white cloths over their arms.

You can sometimes see **mime** (silent) actors in the street. Notice the white make-up on their faces.

At **street bookstalls** you can buy newspapers, magazines, postcards, guide books and even lottery tickets.

The river

This is the **Pont Neuf** or "new bridge". In fact it is the oldest bridge in Paris.

Pont Alexandre III is covered with lamps and statues. It was built in 1900 for a world exhibition.

This **small Statue of Liberty** is on the Pont de Grenelle. The original in New York was built by Eiffel.

What to See and Do in Paris 2

You can get an amazing view of Paris from the steps of the **Sacré Coeur** church, on the hill of Montmartre.

The **Place de la Concorde** is where Louis XVI was guillotined during the Revolution in 1793.

The **Arc de Triomphe** was built to celebrate the victories of Napoleon. The Tomb of the Unknown Soldier is under it.

Notre-Dame was begun in AD1160 and took 200 years to build. The carvings on the doors tell Bible stories.

The **Eiffel Tower** was built in 1889 for a great exhibition. The 320m high tower was the world's tallest building for 40 years.

Thousands of people were imprisoned in the **Conciergerie** before going to the guillotine during the French Revolution. You can still see Marie-Antoinette's cell.

The 19th century **Opéra** is one of the largest theatres in the world. The stage can hold 450 performers.

One of the most famous night-clubs in Paris is the **Moulin Rouge** (Red Windmill). Look for the windmill on the roof.

In the 19th century, many wide, open streets or **boulevards** were built. One of the most famous is the Champs-Élysées.

Paris is still a centre for fashion. Look out for **shops of famous designers,** like Cardin, St Laurent and Dior.

16

Interesting museums

At the **Jeu de Paume** you can see colourful paintings like this one of ballet dancers by Degas. *Métro: Concorde*

The vast **Louvre** museum was once a royal palace. Try to find the armless statue of "Venus de Milo" and Leonardo da Vinci's painting of the "Mona Lisa". *Métro: Louvre or Palais-Royal*

The **Musée Grévin** has life-size wax models of famous people, such as Napoleon and Josephine, in scenes from French history. *Métro: Montmartre*

Weapons and uniforms, including Napoleon's overcoat, are on show at the **Musée de l'Armée**. *Métro: St-François-Xavier*

At the **Musée National des Arts et Traditions Populaires,** you can see objects from everyday life in old France; such as regional costumes, toys, musical instruments, fairground animals and games. *Métro: Sablons*

Go to the **Musée de la Monnaie** to see coins and medals, and, on some days, the workshops of the Mint. *Métro: Pont-Neuf*

The **Palais de la Découverte** is a planetarium and science museum. Look our for the moon rock. *Métro: Franklin-Roosevelt*

The **Musée National des Techniques** has early planes, robots, trains

and clockwork dolls. *Métro: Réaumur-Sébastopol*

17

What to See and Do in Paris 3

The Jardin d'Acclimatation in the Bois de Boulogne has a small zoo, a dolphinarium, donkey rides, puppet shows, miniature cars and a miniature train that leaves from the Porte Maillot. *Métro: Sablons*

Puppet shows are held every afternoon in the Jardin du Luxembourg (off Boulevard St Michel) and the Parc de Choisy. *Métro: Place d'Italie*

You can go **rowing** on the lakes in the Buttes-Chaumont Park *(Métro: Botzaris)* and in the Bois de Boulogne and the Bois de Vincennes.

The biggest **zoo** in Paris is in the Bois de Vincennes *(Métro: Porte Dorée)* open from 9.00 a.m. to 5.30 p.m. Look out for the fake mountain near the bear pit.

You can go **skateboarding** at the Villette Skate Parc *(Métro: Porte de la Villette)* every day but Monday. They will let you hire all the necessary equipment there too.

The Cirque Gruss *(Métro: Rambuteau or Hôtel de Ville)* recreates **circus** acts from old paintings.

The Théâtre du Petit Monde, 252 Faubourg St-Honoré, shows **plays** for children every Wednesday and Saturday.

The Studio Marigny, Carré Marigny cinema (tel. 225 20 74) shows **films** for children all through the year.

Exciting places to go

One of the best ways of seeing Paris is from the river in a **Bateau Mouche**. Boats leave from the Pont de l'Alma, Pont Neuf and Pont d'Iéna.

The **Georges-Pompidou Centre** sometimes has special children's exhibitions. You can have exciting rides on the long escalators which are enclosed in plastic tubes. *Métro: Rambuteau*

On most Saturdays, you can visit the **catacombs** and see millions of old skeletons. Take a torch. *Métro: Denfert-Rochereau.*

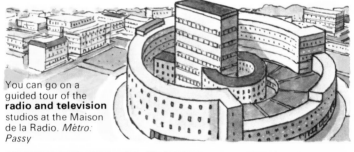

You can go on a guided tour of the **radio and television** studios at the Maison de la Radio. *Métro: Passy*

You can take a **boat trip along the sewers** under Paris on certain days.

Buses and Trains

The easiest way to get about Paris is by underground, the Métro. Trains run about every five minutes, from 5.30 a.m. to 1.15 a.m. There is also an express service (R.E.R.) to the suburbs. Buses run from 6.30 a.m. to 8.30 p.m., and some run until midnight.

This is a **Métro sign.** Look out for the old *Art Nouveau* ones. The 348 métro stations are about 500m apart.

Métro tickets are sold at all stations. There is only one fare. It is cheaper to buy a *"carnet"* of 10 tickets.

There is one **1st class carriage**, painted pale yellow, which stops next to this sign above the platform.

You can use your Métro tickets on **buses** too. Punch your ticket in the machine by the door when you get on the bus. Ring the bell when you want to get off and leave by the doors in the middle of the bus.

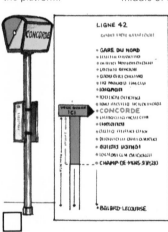

French railways are called the S.N.C.F. You can buy tickets at a station or at a travel agent's. It is best to buy them in advance and to reserve a seat.

All **bus stops** are request stops. The red arrow on the timetable points to where you are on the route. If you are going further than the red section, you need two tickets. Check that you are going in the right direction.

Before you go on to the platform, punch your ticket in one of these machines. An inspector will check and collect it when you are on the train.

On the Road 1

Main roads are called *Routes Nationales*. They all have numbers which are shown on red signposts. Minor roads have yellow signposts. You must always wear a seat belt in a car. Here are some things to look out for when you are travelling on French roads.

The **Citroën Deux Chevaux** (Two Horse-Power) and the **Renault 4** are the two most common types of car in France.

Police Car. Get out of its way as quickly as you can if it is sounding its siren.

Fire Engines. These go to all emergencies, including road accidents.

Ambulance. Most of these are privately owned, often by the local taxi service. They can be very expensive.

Mopeds. You will see lots of people riding these around French towns. You can ride one when you are 14.

Number Plates. The last two numbers show which *département* the car comes from. See page 60 for a number-plate game.

Lorries and caravans have special **speed limit numbers** on the back. The higher one is for motorway driving.

In France, you drive on the right-hand side of the road. This was started by Napoleon's regiment, the Garde Républicaine.

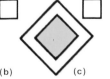

(a)   (b)   (c)

Road Signs. (a) This is a *borne kilométrique*. It shows the distance to nearby towns, and often your height above sea level. (b) Fire signs warn of the danger of fire in dry areas. (c) A yellow diamond shows you have the right of way.

This sign means you must not go faster than 50 k.p.h. Similar round blue signs mean you must not go slower than 50 k.p.h.

On the Road 2

Motorways *(autoroutes)* are numbered – e.g. A6. You usually have to pay a toll *(péage)* to drive along them.

Many péages are automatic. You throw the right amount of coins into the basket, and the barrier rises.

Windsocks on windy stretches of road are to help drivers judge the wind's force and direction.

Many **roads in flat areas are lined with trees.** These provide shade and act as a wind-break. The most common tree are poplars.

Look out for unusual **water towers**. They are usually just outside towns or villages.

Special tall **vineyard tractors** are used in the wine-growing areas to weed between the rows of grape vines.

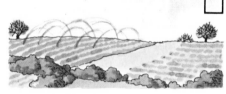

Large areas of farmland have to be kept watered during the summer when there is not much rain. Look out for great shoots of water from large **automatic sprinklers.**

You will often see **wayside crosses and shrines** at the side of the road, especially on old pilgrims' routes.

All towns and villages have a **sign showing the name of the place** as you enter its boundaries. When you leave the town, there is another name sign with a line through it.

22

Villages

There are many different kinds of towns and villages in France. There is often a particular reason why they have been built where they are, such as the need for water or safety. Here are some of the special types of village you might come across.

In the south of France you will see many **hill-top villages**. They were built like this partly to be safe from attack and partly to keep the good soil in the valleys clear for farming.

Fortified towns, called *bastides*, were built during the Middle Ages, when there were many wars. This is Carcassonne, a bastide in South-West France.

The people who built *bastides* gave the same name to many of their towns. Look out for any **towns with these names.** They were all built in the 1200s.

Villages were sometimes built **round a castle or monastery,** which protected the peasants and gave them work. This is Mont-St-Michel in Brittany.

In mountainous regions some villages were built right **at the edge of a cliff,** so that the villagers could spot enemies approaching.

Spa towns, like Évian and Vichy, were built wherever there was a natural spring containing health-giving minerals. The water is often bottled, like this, and sold.

In the past twenty years, many **new towns** have been built, often as an extension to an existing town. Some have strange, modern buildings, like these at Crécy.

23

Towns

Many large modern towns and cities date back to the Middle Ages. If you follow the signs saying *Centre Ville* you will come to the old quarter. Here are some of the things you can look for there.

Wall fortifications, with towers, battlement walks and entrance gates. Often these are ruined.

The old part of the town often has narrow medieval streets, with **half-timbered houses.**

The **town hall** (*Hôtel de Ville*) flies the French flag. Some town halls in the north are very ornate.

Medieval belfry. The bells were rung to warn the citizens of fire or that enemies were approaching.

The **town clock** is often very ornate, a reminder of how important it once was when only rich people could afford a clock.

Old **market halls** are still used in market towns. They usually look like barns with stone pillars.

There is a **square** in the middle of most towns and villages. All the main shops are grouped around it.

Large town houses were often built around a **courtyard** after the 1600s. They were owned by noblemen.

You will see a lot of **wrought-iron balconies** in French towns. They were built at the beginning of the 1900s.

If you get the chance, look into some of the **tiny courtyards** inside buildings. Gardens are often hidden there.

A lot of French people live in flats. A caretaker (**concierge**) looks after all the flats in the block.

Most towns have a decorative **public garden**, with low hedges and a fountain.

In the main square of the town you will often see **statues** of famous people who once lived there.

Policemen in towns are called **agents de police** and wear blue uniforms. They will help you if you get lost.

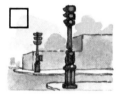
Traffic lights have small lights halfway down the post, so that you can see them more easily from a car.

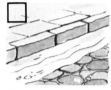
You will sometimes see **water being hosed along the streets** in the morning, to keep them clean.

The **town cemetery** is often just outside the town, away from the church, except in small villages.

At week-ends and on summer evenings, you will often see groups of men playing **boules**. This is a game rather like bowls. The men throw metal balls towards a small marker ball, and points are scored for the balls nearest to the marker. Boules is usually played in a park or square, where the ground is flat.

In small villages, you may still see groups of women doing their washing at a **communal laundry**.

Before houses had running water, the well or **water pump** was an important place in the village.

In the south-west, you may see people playing **pelota**. Men wearing gloves hit a ball against a wall.

Houses 1

Old houses were built out of local materials, and vary in colour according to the type of soil or stone in the area. Here are some different types of houses to spot. Some are in the countryside, some in the towns, so keep your eyes open.

Cave House. In some places, such as the Dordogne a few people live in caves in the chalk hills.

Cob. Made from a mixture of mud paste and straw. One of the oldest kinds of building materials.

You will see **rough stone houses** all over France. Corners, windows and doorways are often outlined in brick or smooth stone.

Tile-hung houses have wooden or slate tiles covering the top storeys. Look out for houses like this in Picardy and northern France.

Whitewash, a mixture of lime and crushed earth or sand, often covers stone houses. Sometimes it is lightly coloured to soften the glare of the sun.

Brick houses are quite rare as it is cheaper to use stone. They are usually larger houses. Corners, doors and windows are usually edged with stone.

Smoothed and neatened stone slabs are used for grander houses in limestone regions, where the stone is softer and cuts easily. Doors and windows are often decorated.

Brick and **stone** are sometimes combined to make a pattern of different colours and shapes. You will see these in Normandy, Béarn and Languedoc.

Wooden houses

Patterned wooden houses like this can be found in Alsace. They usually have lots of balconies and window boxes.

Alpine chalet. The upper storey is made of wooden planks with no windows. Grain is stored up there.

Box-frame houses. The wooden frame is filled in with stone. The downstairs is usually all stone.

Diamond pattern houses have brick or stone filling the spaces in the wooden frame.

Look for this kind of **half-wooden house** in Normandy. Upright pillars of wood are used close together.

Farmhouses

Many French farmhouses have the farm buildings and living rooms under the same roof.

In the big farming areas such as the Languedoc, houses are long and low, with farm buildings attached to the house on either side.

Richer farmers in the north and west of France have their farms arranged around a courtyard. Look out for elaborate gate-posts.

This kind of stone farmhouse has the cellar and stables downstairs. An outside staircase leads to the living rooms.

Crops are stored in the granary in the tall loft of this farmhouse. A ladder or outside staircase leads to the roof.

Look for these little round houses in mountain regions. Farmers use them in summer.

Houses 2

Roofs

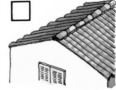

Tall gabled roof, with two steeply sloping sides, so rain runs off easily. See these in the north and mountain regions.

Look for **low gabled roofs,** with gently sloping sides, in the south where there is less rain.

Hipped roofs have slopes on all sides.

Low gabled roofs with jutting out sides are used in snowy places. The snow stays on top and keeps the house warm.

Mansard roofs were originally designed to avoid a tax on windows in the walls.

Overhanging roofs with wooden supports shelter the front of the house. They often jut out over a porch or window.

Gable-ends are often decorative. Look out for these.

Corble-steps or Crow-steps.

Dutch gables have curly edges.

Curved gables look like a moustache.

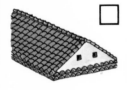

Roman tiles, made from clay, are curved and interlocking. Look for them mainly in Provence.

Flat tiles. Either made from red clay or grey slate. You will usually see them on tall sloping roofs.

Scalloped tiles. Made from slate or wood. They are often on tile-hung houses and curved turret roofs.

Roof decorations

In eastern France, you may see **coloured glazed pottery tiles** made into a pattern like this.

Thatch is made from straw or reeds. In the past, most small farmhouses were covered in thatch.

Thatched roofs often have **flowers** growing along the top. People believed they stopped witches from landing.

Weathercocks. These sometimes indicate the house-owner's job. This is probably a sailor's house.

Look out for **pottery animals** sitting on house roofs.

Pottery vases are sometimes put on the gable-ends.

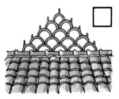

This decoration is called an "**épi**". You will see different designs.

Bouquets de Baptême, are sometimes put up to celebrate the completion of the house.

Sarrasin chimneys, like these, are about 400 years old. You will see them in the Bourgogne area.

Storks sometimes **nest** on the chimney pots in Alsace.

29

Windows and Doorways

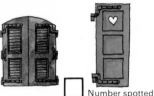

Number spotted

Nearly every house has **shutters** to protect and decorate the windows. They keep out bad weather and the glare of the sun. Here are three different types. See how many you can spot.

Nearly all windows **open inwards.** They are often tall, like doors. This is why glass doors are often called "French windows".

There are often little **balconies** outside, which are used to hang washing out and air the bedding.

Dormer windows, set into the tall sloping roofs, are often quite elaborate. They are sometimes the doors to the granary at the top of the house. Here are three different types to spot.

Look out for **dates, inscriptions** or **sculptures** above the doorways.

A Guardian Angel is often carved above stable doors in Brittany.

In Provence, you will often see a **tall cypress tree** on either side of the doorway. This is a very ancient custom, possibly dating back to Roman times, when it is thought they showed soldiers on the march where to find water.

Some grander houses may have a **coat-of-arms** above the door.

Country Buildings

Many people keep pigeons, which they eat. They are kept in buildings called **pigeonniers,** either near the house, or attached to it like a tower. At one time only the rich lords were allowed to own one, and some of the older ones are quite grand. Look for holes where the birds fly in and out.

Turret pigeon house

Round pigeon house

You will sometimes see little stone huts in the fields. These are called **bories.** They were used to keep sheep and goats in at night.

You will see lots of **goats** in France The farmers put bells round their necks so they can find them easily.

Mills

Watermills have a large wheel which is turned by the flow of a stream. Often the water runs into a millpond.

Very few **windmills** are still in working order. Look for stone or wood ones. Some have thatched roofs. The sails were built so they could be tipped sideways in bad weather to stop them being torn off by strong winds.

Wells

In the past people got their water from **wells.** In some places they are still used by people who do not have taps in their houses. Look for wells in farmyards and village squares. Some have dates carved on them. You will find many that were built about 100 years ago.

Wells are often built of stone with a wooden handle. Sometimes they have roofs to keep the water clean.

Prehistoric France

Stone Age people were living in France over 40,000 years ago, so there are some very old prehistoric remains to be seen.

There are also some superb examples of Roman building left from the time when France was part of the Roman Empire. This map shows where you can see prehistoric and Roman remains.

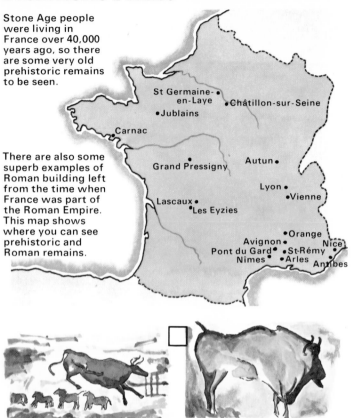

- St Germaine-en-Laye
- Châtillon-sur-Seine
- Jublains
- Carnac
- Grand Pressigny
- Autun
- Lyon
- Lascaux
- Les Eyzies
- Vienne
- Orange
- Avignon
- Nice
- Pont du Gard
- St-Rémy
- Nîmes
- Arles
- Antibes

There are many **cave paintings** in south-western France which are over 40,000 years old. The most famous, found at Lascaux by some children, are no longer open to the public. But there are several other painted caves in the Dordogne which you can visit.

Carvings. Only a few prehistoric tombs in Europe are carved and most of these are in Brittany.

Menhir. Single standing stone, over 4,000 years old. Some are over 6m tall.

Christianized menhir. Christian symbols, such as crosses, were later carved on some menhirs.

Dolmen. Two menhirs covered with a large slab, called a "table stone", which may be up to 6m wide. Probably once a tomb.

Alignment. Lots of menhirs arranged in parallel lines. The most famous are around Carnac, in Brittany. Experts think they may have been used for funeral processions, or by astrologers charting the planets.

Cromlech. Several menhirs grouped together in a circle. Like the alignments, they may have had a religious or astrological use.

Tumulus. Vast, ancient burial chamber, covered over with earth and grass. This one, at Cuniac in Brittany, is 20m high and 260m round.

Things to look for in museums

You can see some very ancient prehistoric objects in French museums. Here are some to look out for. Look out also for things made by the Gauls, who were the people living in France when the Romans invaded. The Gauls were Celtic people who settled in France about 2,000 years ago.

Some of the oldest **flint tools** in Europe have been found in France. See how many different kinds you can find.

See if you can spot a **bone harpoon,** like this one. They were used for fishing.

You may see a **stone carving** or statue like this. This one is the Venus of Laussel, over 10,000 years old.

The Gauls knew how to work **metal.** This gold disk is very elaborate. Look out for simpler things too.

This **pottery** was made by Gauls in northern France. You will see lots of different shapes.

33

Roman France

Julius Caesar invaded France (or Gaul, as it was called then) in 58BC, and it remained part of the Roman Empire for 400 years. The best Roman remains are in the south, where the climate is like that in Italy.

Roman roads were wide and straight, cutting straight across mountains and rivers. Many modern *Routes Nationales* (main roads) follow the same path. This is the stone foundation of a Roman road.

Towers. Roman towns had strong walls, with towers on them. You can still climb the high Tour Magne at Nîmes.

The only way into a walled town was through its **gateway.** This one is the Porte Auguste at Nîmes.

The Romans put up **monuments to celebrate military victories.** This is the Trophée des Alpes, at La Turbie.

Fortified camps housed the Roman legionaries who kept control of the Empire. The best preserved is at Jublains near Evron. It has a high wall with corner towers.

Roman bridges were the only bridges in France until the 1200s. This is the famous Pont du Gard, part of an aqueduct which carried water for 41km from Uzès to Nîmes

Triumphal arches were built to celebrate the military power of Rome. This one is at Orange.

Mausoleums were built as burial places for grand people. There is a specially good one at St-Rémy.

Obelisks were often the markers around which chariot races were run. You can often see them in town squares.

Every Roman city had a **theatre** where plays were acted. This one at Orange is one of the best in Europe, and is particularly famous for the 38m high wall behind the stage. An audience of 7,000 people could watch plays there.

Amphitheatres were where the Romans held chariot races, bull-fights and gladiator fights. In some, you can still go and see bullfights. This one is at Nîmes.

Roman temples were richly carved and decorated. This is the Maison Carrée at Nîmes, a rare example of a Roman building which is not in ruins.

The **Roman town** at Vaison-la-Romaine, near Orange, once had about 20,000 inhabitants. You can see the remains of grand villas, temples and a theatre.

Mosaics like this, made from many small coloured stones, covered the floors of important villas and temples. You will sometimes see them in museums.

Roman ornaments, statues and coins have been dug up all over the south of France. Look for them in local museums.

Look out for French comic strip books about Asterix the Gaul. In them, you can read about the adventures of a village of Gauls who refused to submit to the Romans.

35

Visiting a Château

There are hundreds of châteaux all over France. Here are some of the most famous ones. They are nearly all in the Loire valley, which is where the French kings liked to go hunting. Most are open to the public, at least during the summer.

Ussé looks like a fairy-tale castle. It is said to have inspired the story of the Sleeping Beauty.

Blois. Took hundreds of years to build. It has a famous staircase and a secret poisons cupboard.

Chenonceaux was built in a lake. You can hire rowing boats there and travel through the grounds on a miniature train.

Chambord has a maze of 365 chimneys you can walk round, and also a carriage museum. It is the largest Loire valley château.

Vaux-le-Vicomte (Essonne). Built for Fouquet, Louis XIV's finance minister, who some people say was the "Man in the Iron Mask". His symbol, a squirrel, is all over the house.

Chaumont. Its name means "hot mountain", and it has pictures of volcanoes on the walls. Also famous for its velvet-lined stables.

Langeais is a fortress château with drawbridge, dungeons and ramparts.

Amboise has a balcony where 1,509 people were hanged in 1560. Nearby is the Clos Lucé museum which has models of da Vinci inventions.

Samur fortress château is the home of the *Cadre Noir* riding school. You can watch the riders practising.

Versailles

Versailles (near Paris) was the home of Louis XIV, XV and XVI. It is said that 5,000 servants were needed to run this château because it is so vast.

Hall of Mirrors. Mirrors were so expensive that you had to be very wealthy to own even one. Louis XIV had a whole room lined with them at Versailles.

There are several small houses in the grounds of Versailles. This one is called the **Petit Trianon.**

The Grand Trianon at Versailles is like a small palace. It was built so the king could escape the formal life of court.

At the **Petit Hameau,** Queen Marie Antoinette played at being a shepherdess, and put bows round the lambs' necks.

Château gardens

At many châteaux, you will see **formal gardens,** which were the fashion in the 17th century. Lakes, fountains, hedges and flowerbeds make a huge pattern.

There is often an **orangery,** where you will see orange trees in tubs. Oranges were used to make the house smell nice in the days before there were proper washing facilities.

Low clipped **box hedges** are used to make patterns. Sometimes the pattern is a royal symbol (see page 41).

Look out for neat **cone-shaped trees** that are so tidy they look artificial. They are real trees, carefully trimmed.

There are often spectacular **fountains.** The Versailles ones are working on some Sundays in summer.

What to Look for in a Château 1

The name château means "castle", but, though the early ones have strong defences, most are grand houses built in more peaceful times. Here are some examples of how building styles changed over the years. When you see a château, try to date it from its style.

1000s Square Donjon. Thick stone walls, narrow arrow slits. Entrance on an upper floor.

1100s Round Donjon. Easier to defend than square donjon, because no corners for enemy to hide round.

1200s Donjon surrounded by a courtyard, called a bailey, and a strong stone wall. Sometimes there are two or three baileys and walls.

1300s Final development of fortress château. Large but compact building with inner courtyard, turrets, battlement walks and arrow slits.

1400s Gradual change from fortress to country house. Outer walls still have the look of a fortress, but walls facing courtyard have larger windows, and decoration. Tall roofs.

1500s (Renaissance Style). Corner turrets for decoration only. Dormer windows in roof, decorated chimneys, pillars and open walkways.

Early 1600s (Louis XIII Style). Pink or red brick with white stone facings around windows, doorways and corners. No turrets.

Late 1600s (Early Classical Style). Corner "pavilions" at each end of house. Plainer style, tall roofs – often domed – and larger windows.

1700s (Classical Style). Less carving and decoration. Lots of windows, flat roof with balustrades and ornamental vases, pillars and columns.

1800s Little that was new, but drew on ideas from past years, and so often a mixture of styles. This house has a tall roof of 1600s and front of 1700s.

Things to spot in châteaux

Here are some things to look out for when you visit a château. Many châteaux were added to and changed over the years, so you are likely to see things built at different times in the same place.

Drawbridge. A bridge across the moat which could be raised when enemies approached.

Watch turrets. Small round rooms sticking out from top of wall, where look-outs could watch for enemies.

Machicolations. Holes below the battlements through which missiles and boiling tar could be dropped on attackers.

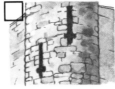

Arrow slits. Narrow openings in walls, through which arrows could be shot, while archers remained safe.

Sloping walls at the bottom of towers made it harder for enemies to attack with battering rams and ladders.

Murder holes in the ceiling of the gateway were also for dropping things like boiling tar on to enemies.

Cross bows were the most common weapons in the 1400s. You may see them hung on walls.

Suit of armour. Worn to protect men when they went into battle. Notice how short many of them are.

What to Look for in a Château 2

The direction of most **spiral staircases** allows someone defending the stairs from above to have his sword arm free.

Tapestries were used to decorate walls and to keep draughts out. They were often made specially for the house and show Bible scenes, myths or historical events.

Inside walls were often covered with **patterned leather** to keep out the damp.

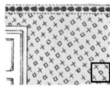

Silk wall-hangings were changed every season. Red in winter, green in spring, white in summer, gold in autumn.

Later châteaux have **painted and moulded wall and door panels.** Lots of gold paint was used.

Painted wooden ceilings with exposed beams and geometric patterns are quite common.

Coffered ceilings have carved and painted wooden panels sunk into a wooden framework. Usually in grand rooms.

Paintings on the ceilings are sometimes by famous artists. Some appear to be three-dimensional.

Four poster beds had thick curtains to keep out draughts and screen the occupants from people passing through the room.

You will sometimes see a **travelling chest** like this, with secret compartments for documents and jewels.

Red Indian heads were carved on the legs of many pieces of furniture after the discovery of America in 1492.

In many châteaux you can see the vast kitchens where meals were prepared for thousands of people. Look out for **copper cooking pans**.

The larger châteaux were like small villages and had everything the occupants needed, including a private **chapel** like this one.

The owners of the château

Look for symbols above doors, windows and fireplaces.

Initials. See how many different ones you can find.

The **family's crest,** in this case a squirrel, may be carved in wood, painted or embroidered on tapestries.

Rich people often had their **portraits** painted so you can see what the former inhabitants looked like.

Symbols of kings and queens

Many kings and queens had their own symbols and you will see them, not only in their own châteaux, but also in those of loyal nobles. Only in royal houses, though, will you see symbols with crowns above them.

A **porcupine** was the symbol of Louis XII (1498–1515).

A **Franciscan girdle with ermine tufts** became Anne of Brittany and Charles VIII's symbol when they married in 1491.

A **salamander** was the crest of François I (1515–1547).

Anne of Brittany and her daughter Claude had an **ermine** as their symbol.

The **Sun King,** Louis XIV, used this symbol (1643–1715).

The Bourbon royal family symbol was the **fleur de lys** (1589–1610).

Churches

Here are some of the different types of church buildings you will see in France. When you visit churches, remember you should wear decent clothes – not shorts or bathing costumes. You can visit a few monasteries, but most prefer you to write and make arrangements first.

Basilica. Modelled on Roman law-court buildings. Usually built over the tomb of a saint.

Baptistery. A separate building from the main church, used for baptizing people into the Christian religion.

Abbey or monastery. Home of a community of monks. An abbey is a monastery ruled by an abbot. The monks were wealthy and powerful in the Middle Ages and were responsible for the building of many churches.

A **cathedral** is a church ruled by a bishop. The bishop's throne used to be called the **cathedra**.

Bridge chapels. Travellers prayed for a safe journey in these. and left money for the upkeep of the bridge.

Fortified churches, which look like castles, were built during the Middle Ages when there were many religious wars.

Rock-pinnacle churches. You will sometimes see churches like this in mountainous regions, like the Auvergne.

Enclosures. You will see these in Brittany. They consist of a triumphal arch leading to a cemetery, a church, an ossuary (where bones are kept) and a calvary, which is a large carved stone cross. Many were built during the plague in 1598.

Domed churches, like those in Eastern Europe, are sometimes found in southern France.

Things to spot in churches

Despite many religious wars, the Roman Catholic Church has been strong in France since the Middle Ages. In the 1100s, there was even a pope in France who lived in Avignon. Here are some things to look out for in Roman Catholic churches.

Holy water stoop. On entering a church, people bless themselves by making the sign of the cross with holy water.

Each chapel inside the church is dedicated to a saint. People **light a candle** for each prayer they make to the saint.

Pilgrims still visit churches where there are relics of a saint, in the hope that they will be helped or cured. There are special saints to help with different problems. Holy places like Lourdes are also visited by pilgrims.

Reliquary. A box, shaped like a church or a hollow statue, in which relics, often bones, of a saint are kept.

The **confessional** is a box where people confess their sins to a priest, who cannot see them.

The **choir screen** encloses the choir which is where the priests pray. It is often richly carved.

Misericord. Small carved perch on the back of a choir stall, on which the priests can rest.

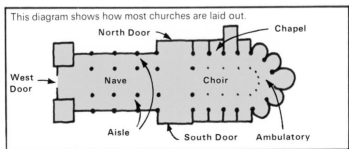

This diagram shows how most churches are laid out.

North Door

Chapel

West Door

Nave

Choir

Aisle

South Door

Ambulatory

Finding out the Age of a Church

Different styles of church building were introduced as technical knowledge increased. Here you can see the main features of each period of architecture. See if you can spot them when you visit a church.

Front view

Back view

Romanesque (1000s–1100s). Builders borrowed many ideas from earlier Roman buildings. Quite squat, with a few small windows set in thick stone walls. Rounded arches on windows, doors and vaults.

Gothic (1100s–1400s). Tall building, many windows, pointed arches. Lots of flying buttresses.

Renaissance (1500s). Use of Italian ideas of architecture. Rounder arches, pillars and ornate decoration.

Classical (1600s). Domed roof rather than tower. Plainer style, straight pillars and windows.

Towers

Romanesque. Low, 8-sided or square. Pyramid roof.

Gothic Tower. Square, often with 8-sided upper level.

Gothic spire. Small square tower, with tall narrow spire.

Renaissance Bell Tower. Small domed top with lantern.

Doorways

Romanesque. Rounded arch with many carvings round it.

Gothic. Pointed arch. Many sculptures. The "tympanum" (space inside arch, above the door) is often carved.

Renaissance. Usually two separate doors under one very high tympanum.

44

Ceilings

Romanesque **barrel vault.** Rounded vault with a series of exposed arches.

Romanesque **oven vault.** A quarter of a sphere forms the roof of the small chapels in the church.

Late Romanesque **groin vault.** Two overlapping barrel vaults. Cannot see the arches.

Gothic **rib vault.** Many tall pointed arches, meeting at a centre point.

Renaissance **lantern vault.** Pendulums hang from the centre of the vault.

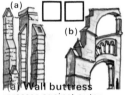

(a) **Wall buttress** presses against outer wall to give support.
(b) **Flying buttress** stands away from wall. Gives even greater support.

Windows

Romanesque. Small rounded arch on top. Side pillars and plain glass.

Early Gothic Lancet style. Narrow, slightly pointed arch.

Radiant Gothic. Tall pointed arch. Circle pattern.

Flamboyant Gothic. Tall pointed arch. Flame-like pattern.

Renaissance. Tall with round arch. Little ironwork decoration.

Rose Wheel

Radiant Rose

Flamboyant Rose

Rose windows are often seen in French Gothic cathedrals, usually above the west door. Their pattern is similar to that of the other windows.

45

Church Decorations

Many churches were built in the days before most people could read or write. They were decorated with pictures in stone or glass, which told stories from the Bible or of the lives of the saints. Here are some examples of where to look for picture stories.

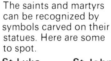

Capital

Capitals are at the top of pillars. They are usually carved. Romanesque capitals have designs of leaves, flowers, geometric patterns and often sinister monsters. Gothic capitals have small scenes from the Bible.

 (a)

 (b)

 (c)

Look for **medallions** on either side of the west door. They show:

(a) Virtues and vices. This is the sin of cowardice – an armed man is running from a hare.

(b) Signs of the Zodiac. This is the ram of Aries.

(c) Seasons. Here you can see the harvest time.

Stained glass often has biblical scenes. Usually found only in Gothic or later churches.

Gargoyles on church roofs were supposed to frighten away evil spirits. Also used as rain water spouts.

The saints and martyrs can be recognized by symbols carved on their statues. Here are some to spot.

St Luke (angel)   St John (eagle)

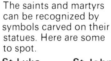

St Mark (lion)   St Matthew (bull)

St Peter holds the keys of heaven.

St Paul holds the sword which killed him.

John the Baptist holds a lamb.

St James has a cockle shell and a pilgrim's staff.

St Sebastian is pierced by arrows.

Painted vaults. Originally churches were completely painted inside. Most of the colours have faded or disappeared now, but you may be lucky and see a ceiling which is still painted.

Frescoes are pictures painted straight onto the wet plaster of the walls. They were often used in churches, especially in the south.

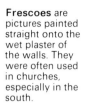

Look out for a **pulpit fixed to the wall.** These often have carvings, or even statues, on the roof. See if you can find a staircase for the priest to climb up.

Dog

Lion

Tombs. A dog at the feet of a figure on a tomb means the person died peacefully. A lion means the person was killed in battle.

See if you can spot an ornate **ironwork bell-cage** on the roof of the church tower, especially in the south of France.

When a **cardinal** died, his **hat** was often hung from the roof of the church. You can still see them sometimes, for instance at Beauvais.

Dead Men's Lantern. Often found near cemeteries in the south-west. The light was to keep watch over the dead, and guide pilgrims on their way.

Coloured stone **mosaics** often decorate the floors of churches. This one, at Chartres Cathedral, shows a maze through which sinners had to walk.

47

Fun Things to Do 1

Zoos and safari parks

The *Syndicat d'Initiative* (Tourist Office) in the town where you are staying will give you lists of things to see and do nearby. Look out for posters advertising things too. The next few pages suggest what sort of things to look out for.

This is the **Safari Park** at Thot in the Périgord. Here you can see bison, wild boar and other animals similar to those in the prehistoric wall paintings found in the caves of the area.

In the park around the Château de Thoiry-en-Yvelines, 40km west of Paris, you can see over 800 **wild animals** from Africa and Asia roaming free.

There are **bird sanctuaries** in many parts of France. Le Parc Ornithologique at Villars Les Dombes, (Ain) has over 200 species of birds.

At the top of the steps leading to the Royal Palace of Monaco in Monte Carlo, there is a huge **aquarium** full of different varieties of tropical fish.

At the **Marineland Dolphinarium** on the Côte d'Azur you can watch dolphins and a killer whale dance and do acrobatics. The show is floodlit at night.

Adventure playgrounds

In the **deer park** at Jonchery-sur-Vesle, (Aisne) there is a children's adventure playground, where you will find lots of things to play with.

You can become a Red Indian for a day at this **Indian village** in the Vallée des Peaux Rouges (Valley of the Red Indians) north of Paris.

National parks

In each region of France, large areas of beautiful countryside have been turned into *parcs nationaux* (national parks), where the land and animals are protected. Most of the parks are uninhabited and they are good places to go walking, pony-trekking, canoeing, fishing, cycling and rock climbing.

The Camargue is one of the national parks. It is a large area of marshland across the Rhône delta. Lots of animals and birds, such as beavers and flamingoes, live there. The Camargue is famous for its wild, white horses and black bulls. Look out for horsemen carrying pronged sticks rounding them up.

Caves

At the Gouffre du Padirac. Gramat, Lot, you can go on a **boat tour along an underground river** through caves up to 100m high. The caves are illuminated, and you can see gigantic stalactites which are centuries old.

Circuses

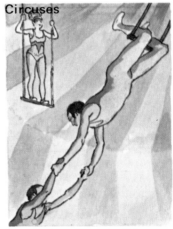

Look out for posters advertising travelling **circuses.** You can see performing animals and flying trapeze acts, which were invented by a French acrobat called Léotard in 1859.

Fun Things to Do 2

Highly skilled people still practise many of the traditional crafts in France. Factories and workshops, where you can see how things are made, are often open to the public. Here are some places you can visit.

At the Chocolaterie Poulin, Blois (Loire-et-Cher), you can watch **chocolates** being made.

There are small **potteries** all over France, especially in Provence and Alsace, which you can visit.

At Biot in Provence you can visit the **glassworks** (*verrerie*) to see how glass is blown and cut. Every month they make a different coloured glass.

Le Musée Historique du Papier at Ambert in the Auvergne is really an old **paper factory**. You can watch the traditional methods of making paper by hand.

Grasse, Provence, is the centre of the French **perfume** industry. At the Fragonard factory you can see how the oil for perfume is extracted from flowers.

At Roquefort in the Languedoc you can visit the cellars where the smelly blue-veined **Roquefort cheeses** are left to mature. They are made from ewes' milk.

The Chinon-Richelieu Railway. In the summer you can travel on the small vintage **steam train** from Chinon to the **model village** of Richelieu (Indre-et-Loire).

The **funicular (cable) railway** from St Hilaire-du-Touret in the Savoie climbs up a mountain side and is the steepest climbing railway in Europe.

Wine-making

The main wine producing regions of France are Burgundy, Bordeaux, Alsace, the Rhône and Champagne. Look out for roads through the wine regions marked *Route du Vin*. These take you past the main vineyards. The best time of year to visit them is early autumn.

When you are driving through vineyards, look out for signs saying *Salons de Dégustation* or *Visitez les Caves*. In any of these places you can visit the cellars where the wine is made. You can also taste some of the wines.

Champagne cellars are huge. At Mercier in Épernay there is a small train to take you around them.

In Burgundy people taste wine from a "taste-vin" like this, so they can see its colour more easily.

In the old houses at Riquewihr in Alsace you can see old wine presses and huge, decorated casks.

In the evenings from early summer until the autumn you can see Son et Lumière (Sound and Light) performances at many historic houses and churches. The performance of acting, music and lightshow takes you through the history of the place. Here you can see the Son et Lumière pageant at one of the Loire valley châteaux.

Fun Things to Do 3

There are lots of interesting museums in France. Most areas have a folklore museum, where you can see how people used to live. There are also museums with unusual collections. Here are some ideas for different museums you could visit.

Toy museums

Le Musée du Jouet, Poissy, (Ile de France). In this museum you can see about 500 different **toys and games** from the 1800s. In one room you can even find out how they were made.

Musée National de Monaco. This Museum contains a collection of **clockwork dolls** from the 1700s and 1800s. The dolls are in period costume. You can watch them in action and see a display showing how they were made.

Musée Gadagne, Lyon, (Rhône). In this **puppet museum** you can see the history of the famous Guignol puppets, the French version of Punch and Judy.

Musée d'Allard, Montbrison, (Loire). This collection shows the history of **dolls** from all over the world. The oldest doll is over 3000 years old.

Musée de Champlitte, (Haute-Saône). Reconstructed **interiors of houses,** farms and shops show you how people once lived in this region of France.

Musée Basque, Bayonne, is a **folklore museum.** It has interiors of local houses, farm machines, costumes and games.

Transport museums

Musée de l'Automobile, Le Mans, (Sarthe). On the famous 24 hour race track at Le Mans you can see a collection of 140 **cars** made between 1884 and 1970.

Château Lannessan, Cussac, Aquitaine. This is a museum of **horse-drawn vehicles**. You can see carriages and harnesses and visit the old stables.

Le Musée de l'Automobile, Rochetaillée-sur-Saône. This museum has a collection of **vintage cars** which are still in good working order.

Balloon Museum, Balleroy, Normandy. In this museum you can trace the history of **hot-air balloons** and see how they work.

Other interesting museums

Musée des Beaux Arts, Besançon. In the clock department of this museum you can see old **clocks,** sundials and the most complicated watch in the world.

Musée du Phonographe, Sainte-Maxime (Var). Here you can trace the history of **gramophones** and see many old barrel organs, pianolas and musical boxes.

The **Bayeux tapestry** is in a house next to the cathedral at Bayeux in Normandy. The tapestry is 70m long and shows, in 58 brightly coloured scenes, how William the Conqueror invaded England in 1066. It used to hang in Bayeux Cathedral and was probably embroidered in England.

Sports

If you are interested in sport, there are lots of things you can see or do while you are in France. All French towns have good sports facilities in their *Stade Municipale*, and anyone can use them at low cost. Here are some sports you can watch or try yourself.

Cycling is a good way to explore an area you do not know. You can hire bicycles from the railway station in most towns and from some cycle shops. Remember to ride on the right and give way to traffic coming from the right.

The French play **tennis** all the year round. The tourist office will give you a list of tennis courts you can hire in the area where you are staying.

Ice skating is popular in France and you can go skating in most towns. You will be able to hire skates at the ice rink, which is called *la patinoire*.

In the winter you can go **cross-country skiing** *(ski-de-fond)* in hilly areas. It is great fun and you do not need any experience.

Amateur, 15-a-side **rugby union** is popular in France, especially in Aquitaine and Languedoc. You can watch matches every Saturday during the winter.

You can watch **soccer** matches in most towns every Saturday from August to May. The French Cup Final, the highlight of the season, is held in Paris in June.

The big sporting events

The **24 Heures du Mans** is a 24 hour car race at Le Mans, Sarthe. It is one of the most famous car races in the world and takes place at the end of spring every year.

The **Monte Carlo Rally** is held every January. Rally drivers set off from all over Europe and meet in the South of France to race through the streets of Monte Carlo, in Monaco.

The **Tour de France** is a cycling race round France, which begins in June and ends in July. The route is split into 22 laps and covers about 4,000km. It ends in Paris.

The **Prix de l'Arc de Triomphe** is a famous horse race, which is held every autumn at the Longchamp race track outside Paris. The prize money is the highest in Europe for a horse race.

Festivals and Carnivals 1

There are many festivals in France. Some celebrate religious occasions, others historical events or even just a good harvest. Here are some of the special festivals and traditions.

On 14 July everyone in France celebrates the storming of the Bastille prison at the beginning of the French Revolution. Houses are decorated with flags and garlands, there are torchlit processions, military parades and firework displays, and people dance in the streets until dawn.

On **Christmas Eve** children put out shoes, rather than stockings, for Father Christmas to fill with gifts.

The traditional **Christmas** pudding is the Bûche de Noel, a cake shaped like a yule log and coated in chocolate.

In Provence, people take live lambs to church at **Christmas** time and lay them at the foot of the crib.

On **6 December** people in the north and east of France celebrate the Fête de St Nicolas (Santa Claus), the patron saint of children. In many towns you can see a man dressed as a bishop walking through the streets with a donkey and handing out sweets and chocolates to children.

At midnight on **New Year's Eve** (Saint-Sylvestre), people in cars all sound their car horns as loudly as they can to celebrate the new year.

On **6 January** the French celebrate la Fête des Rois (festival of the three kings). People eat a special cake, and the person who finds the bean hidden in it is King of the Day.

After a **Christening** the guests and children outside the church are given small bags of pink or blue sugared almonds, called dragées.

In villages, especially on Saturdays, you might see a **bride and groom** walking down the street with children holding flowers above their heads.

On special days like Christmas, there are often **skiing displays** in the mountains. Ski guides ski down the mountains at night carrying flaming torches.

In northern France huge models of local historical or legendary heroes, called **Les Géants** (the giants) are paraded through the streets on festive occasions.

Festivals and Carnivals 2

The **carnival at Nice** is the biggest in France. It lasts for 12 days and ends on Shrove Tuesday (le Mardi Gras). The whole town is lit up and people line the streets to watch colourful processions go by. You can join in a battle of flowers with the people on floats and watch fireworks being let off over the sea.

On **1 May** people give their friends bunches of lilies of the valley, to bring them good luck.

Flower festivals, like the Jasmin Festival at Grasse, are held in all the big flower-growing areas in the summer. Floats covered with flowers file through the streets, and people throw flowers at each other.

Many areas in France have their own special **religious festivals.** You may see processions of pilgrims in traditional costume.

On the **Pfiffertag** (piper's day) in Ribeauvillé, Alsace, people in traditional costume dance through the streets of the village carrying a giant cake.

Les Vendanges (grape harvest). In the big wine producing areas the local people celebrate the end of the grape harvest every autumn. They hold big dances and taste the new wine. Members of the old wine societies dress up in their traditional costume.

Basque Festivals. The Basque region in south-west France has special traditions of its own. All through the year you can go to lively festivals of Basque dancing and watch traditional hobby-horse and sword dances.

Bullfighting. A lot of bulls are bred in the South of France and you can go to bull fights in towns such as Nîmes and Arles. In the summer you can also watch bull-chasing, which is very popular and where the bulls are not killed.

Many towns have **fun fairs** during the summer with fireworks and decorated floats. You will see posters advertising them. Look on page 61 for the French words for fair and fireworks. At Chinon, in the Loire valley, in August, there is a medieval festival with acrobats, jugglers and fire-eaters.

Car Number-Plate Game

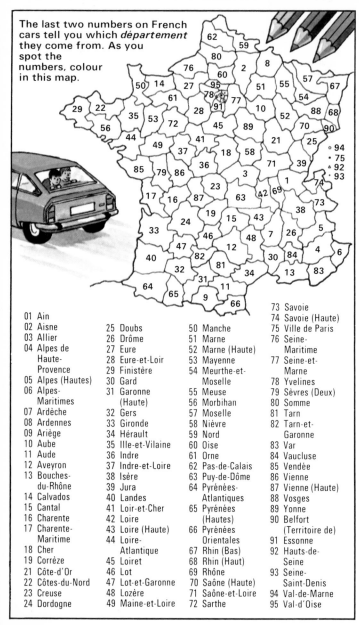

The last two numbers on French cars tell you which *département* they come from. As you spot the numbers, colour in this map.

01 Ain	25 Doubs	50 Manche
02 Aisne	26 Drôme	51 Marne
03 Allier	27 Eure	52 Marne (Haute)
04 Alpes de Haute- Provence	28 Eure-et-Loir	53 Mayenne
	29 Finistère	54 Meurthe-et- Moselle
05 Alpes (Hautes)	30 Gard	55 Meuse
06 Alpes- Maritimes	31 Garonne (Haute)	56 Morbihan
	32 Gers	57 Moselle
07 Ardèche	33 Gironde	58 Nièvre
08 Ardennes	34 Hérault	59 Nord
09 Ariège	35 Ille-et-Vilaine	60 Oise
10 Aube	36 Indre	61 Orne
11 Aude	37 Indre-et-Loire	62 Pas-de-Calais
12 Aveyron	38 Isère	63 Puy-de-Dôme
13 Bouches- du-Rhône	39 Jura	64 Pyrénées- Atlantiques
14 Calvados	40 Landes	65 Pyrénées (Hautes)
15 Cantal	41 Loir-et-Cher	
16 Charente	42 Loire	66 Pyrénées Orientales
17 Charente- Maritime	43 Loire (Haute)	67 Rhin (Bas)
	44 Loire- Atlantique	68 Rhin (Haut)
18 Cher	45 Loiret	69 Rhône
19 Corrèze	46 Lot	70 Saône (Haute)
21 Côte-d'Or	47 Lot-et-Garonne	71 Saône-et-Loire
22 Côtes-du-Nord	48 Lozère	72 Sarthe
23 Creuse	49 Maine-et-Loire	
24 Dordogne		

73 Savoie
74 Savoie (Haute)
75 Ville de Paris
76 Seine- Maritime
77 Seine-et- Marne
78 Yvelines
79 Sèvres (Deux)
80 Somme
81 Tarn
82 Tarn-et- Garonne
83 Var
84 Vaucluse
85 Vendée
86 Vienne
87 Vienne (Haute)
88 Vosges
89 Yonne
90 Belfort (Territoire de)
91 Essonne
92 Hauts-de- Seine
93 Seine- Saint-Denis
94 Val-de-Marne
95 Val-d'Oise

Useful Addresses

The French Government Tourist Office (FGTO) will supply lists of hotels and campsites and details of tours. They also provide booklets on each region of France, and the addresses of local tourist offices. If you speak some French, ask for a booklet called *Loisirs en France*. This tells you many interesting things you can do on holiday in France.
French Government Tourist Office, 178 Piccadilly, London W1V 0AL. tel: (01) 491 2516.

For general information on France, contact the Cultural Service of the French Embassy.
French Embassy (Cultural Service), 22 Wilton Crescent, London SW1. tel: (01) 235 8080.

Where to stay and how to get there

The Youth Hostels Association and the books listed below will also tell you where you can stay.
Youth Hostels Association (YHA), 14 Southampton Street, London WC2. tel: (01) 836 8541.
French Farm and Village Holiday Guide (Duo Publishing).
Campsites in France (Letts).

For general information on travelling in France, contact a travel agent or the French Railways, or look out for the Michelin maps listed below.
French Railways, 179 Piccadilly, London W1V 0BA. tel: (01) 493 9731/4451.
989 France (road map)
915 France Main Roads/Atlas
400 France Motorways/Atlas.

Guide books and phrase books

The Michelin green tourist guides are probably the best basic guide books to France. Each one deals with a different region and gives you general information about the area, as well as suggesting interesting places to visit and good routes to take. Some other guide books are listed below.
You will have much more fun on holiday if you can speak some French. You will find a phrase book very useful.
Letts go to France (Letts).
The Young Traveller's Guide to France (Duo Publishing).
French Riviera (Berlitz).
Loire Valley (Berlitz).
Junior Guide to French (Usborne)

Some useful French words

castle	**flea market**	**park**
le château	*le marché aux puces*	*le jardin public*
ler shattoh	ler marshay oh pewss	ler jardang pewbleek
church	**glassworks**	**pottery**
l'église	*la verrerie*	*la poterie*
leggleez	lah vaireree	lah potree
circus	**guide book**	**swimming pool**
le cirque	*le guide*	*la piscine*
ler seerk	ler geed	lah peeseen
exhibition	**market**	**tennis court**
l'exposition	*le marché*	*le terrain de tennis*
lekspozeesyong	ler marshay	ler terrang der teneess
fair	**monastery**	**wine cellars**
la fête foraine	*le monastère*	*les caves*
lah fet foren	ler monastair	lay kahv
fireworks	**museum**	**zoo**
les feux d'artifice	*le musée*	*le jardin zoologique*
lay fer darteefeess	ler mewzay	ler jardang zo-olojeek

Index